To my mother Irene P.

DIMITRIOS PANDERMALIS

THE ARCHAEOLOGICAL SITE AND THE MUSEUM

DION

THE ARCHAEOLOGICAL SITE AND THE MUSEUM

DION

DIMITRIOS PANDERMALIS

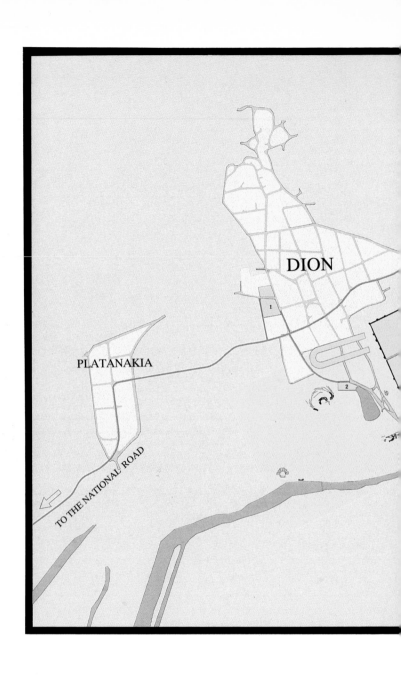

DION

PLATANAKIA

TO THE NATIONAL ROAD

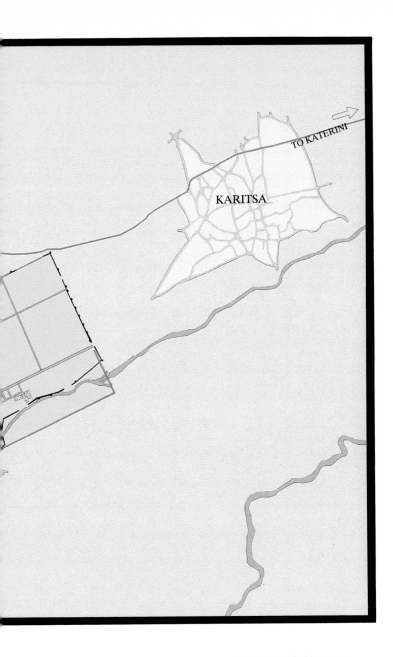

1. Archaeological Museum
2. Entrance to archaeological site

DION IN THE ANCIENT SOURCES

When singing of the divine love of Zeus and Thyia, daughter of Deukalion, the forefather of the Greeks, Hesiod tells us, about 700 BC, that she became pregnant and gave birth to two children, Magnes and Makedon, who lived in Pieria around Mount Olympos. The site sacred to Zeus in this area was Dion in the foothills of Olympos. The first mention of the city of Dion occurs in the description of the advance of the Spartan general Brasidas from Thessaly to the land of his friend Perdikkas II, king of Macedonia. It was the first city that Brasidas came to after crossing the borders in the summer of 424 BC. According to the same author, Archelaos, who ascended to the throne of Macedonia towards the end of the 5th c. BC, reorganised the state, strengthened the central authority, built roads and fortresses, and modernised the army. According to Diodoros and other writers, he organised athletic and dramatic contests lasting nine days at Dion in honour of Olympian Zeus and the Muses, who were worshipped there. The plays presented will certainly have included the *Archelaos* and the *Bacchae*, written by Euripides during the last years of his life at the Macedonian court. Dio Chrysostom asserts that Philip and Alexander used to celebrate their victories at Dion with impressive sacrifices to Zeus and the Muses, and by holding the Olympic games.

Left: Aerial photograph of the south entrance to the city and the Great Baths.

Part of an inscription from the sanctuary of Zeus.

According to Diodoros, it was at Dion that Alexander celebrated the preparations for his famous campaign by making splendid sacrifices to Zeus the Olympian father, organising competitions and holding brilliant receptions in his tent, which held one hundred couches. Many ancient authors speak of the masterpiece carved by Lysippos at Alexander's orders, which was erected at Dion. It depicted the 25 mounted companions of Alexander who fell at the battle of Granikos. These bronze statues were later taken to Rome by Metellus. The special affection in which Alexander held Dion is also clear from the desire expressed in his will that a luxurious temple of Zeus should be erected there.

During the reign of Philip V, there was a devastating raid on Dion by the Aetolians, which is described by Polybios. The Aetolian general Skopas razed the city walls, houses and gymnasium, burned the stoas and other buildings within the precinct of Zeus, and buried the statues of the Macedonian kings in the earth.

The city was rebuilt and when in 169 BC the consul M. Philippus captured it, he admired its fortifications, public buildings and the vast number of statues. Our source for this, Livy, adds that the Roman consul showed great respect for the sanctuary of Zeus, taking care personally to protect it from the hands of his soldiers.

The last reference to Dion, which dates from the 10th c. AD, occurs in the work by Constantine Porphyrogennetos, *De Thematibus*.

From the Renaissance onwards, the site of the city is marked on maps as *Dium* or *Stadia*, meaning 'at Dium'. The modern inhabitants call the fortified city 'the castle', which indeed it was in early Christian times.

Left: Part of the map by Giacomo Cantelli (1690).

The History Of The Excavations

Drawing of the leg of the marble couch with painted decoration in Macedonian Tomb I.

Dion enters the archaeological bibliography in the 19th c. through the book by the English officer W M Leake, *Travels in Northern Greece III*. 1835. On 21st of December 1806, Leake visited the ruins near the village of Malathria, identified the fortifications, theatre, stadium, a temple and a tumulus, and wrote that he had no doubt at all that this was the famous Dion, one of the outstanding cities of Macedonia. Dion was later visited by the French Archaeologist L Heuzey, in 1855 and 1861, and immediately after the liberation of the region from the Turks, Professor G P Ikonomos published the ancient inscriptions of Dion. Excavations began in 1928, when the Vice-chancellor of the University of Thessaloniki, G Sotiriadis, decided to investigate Dion, since in his opinion it was the most promising of all the sites in Macedonia. Sotiriadis sank a large number of trial trenches in search of the sanctuary of Zeus. His most important discovery was a Macedonian tomb of the late 4th c. BC , which had a Doric facade, an Ionic antechamber and a spacious burial chamber. The same excavator also located one of the earliest Christian basilicas in the city of Dion. This first brief excavation period came to an end in 1931. Investigations were resumed, after an interval of more than thirty years, by professor G Bakalakis, who excavated part of the 4th c. BC defensive enceinte and a

second c. AD theatre.

In 1973 began a new excavation period, directed by Professor D Pandermalis. Pride of place in the investigation went to the area of the sanctuaries, followed by that of the urban centre, the city cemetery and the tumulus cemetery, in the foothills of the mountain, which yielded finds dating from the Early Iron Age. In 1983 Dion acquired an archaeological museum, thanks to the personal interest of the then president of the Greek Republic, K Karamanlis. The on-going excavation by the University of Thessaloniki is one of the largest in Greece, and offers undergraduates and newly graduated students many opportunities to gain experience of modern excavation techniques.

The archaeological museum of Dion, set amidst pine trees.

Drawing of the battle scene painted on the marble crosspiece of the couch in Macedonian Tomb I.

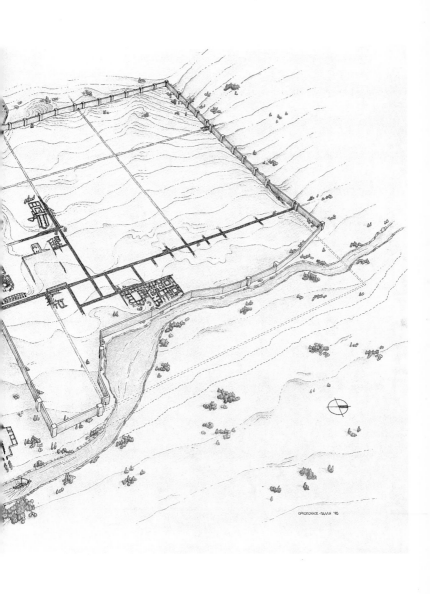

Dion: The sanctuares
and the city.

THE ARCHAEOLOGICAL SITE

F rom the building at the entrance to the archaeological site, a paved path leads to the sanctuary of Demeter, passing a small lake which has an abundance of spring water. A few ancient objects and some large tree-trunks were recovered from the bottom of this lake. There seems to have been a sizeable spring at this site from very early times, which suggested that the area of the cult of the Muses should be sought in this region.

The **Sanctuary of Demeter**, which is approached from its west side, contains some of the earliest known sacred buildings, and the earliest object yielded by the excavations – a Mycenaean seal-ring dating from the 15th c. BC – was found here. These buildings, which date from the 6th c. BC, have the form of a *megaron*, that is, they are long, narrow buildings with a deep antechamber. They were constructed of well-fitted stones and unbaked bricks. Inside were wooden benches on which were placed dedications: terracotta figurines,

Left: Aerial photograph of the sanctuary of Demeter.

Finger-ring with a depiction of a lion.

Model of the main temples in the sanctuary of Demeter.

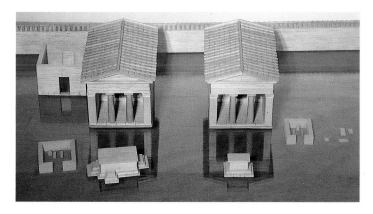

The head of the cult statue of Demeter.

jewellery, lamps and small vases. In the late 4th c. BC these buildings were replaced by two Doric temples *in antis*. Sacrificial altars were erected at the east. Inside the temples were found the bases of the cult statues, and in one of them a marble head of Demeter, carved in the late 4th c. BC, came to light. The identity of the cult is confirmed by an inscription scratched on the base of a vase, which mentions the name of this same goddess. In the Classical period some small, single-roomed temples were built near the main temples, with

1,2. Archaic megara
3,4. Hellenistic temples

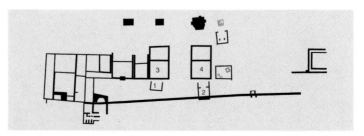

Statue of Aphrodite from the sanctuary of Demeter.

Statue of a girl wearing a peplos from the sanctuary of Demeter.

stone tables in front of the cult statue. On these tables were placed the first-fruits of the harvest. One such small temple was probably devoted to the worship of Baubo, who, with her lewd jokes, succeeded in cheering up the grieving Demeter after the loss of Persephone. Next to the temple of Demeter there was a well contemporary with it inside a built enclosure-wall, and a further two wells, with clay walls, were found at a lower level. This was probably a local imitation of the Kallichoros well, the sacred spring at Eleusis.

The sanctuary of Demeter is the earliest excavated so far in Macedonia, and it continued to function without break until the 4th c. AD

The Sanctuary of
Demeter in the
Classical period.

Visitors now proceed to the east. Crossing the wooden bridge over the river they come to the **sanctuary of Isis**. The river bed was dug in the 1950s. The ancient bed was clearly some distance to the east. The river at Dion was famous in antiquity not only because it was navigable, as Pausanias informs us, but because it was closely connected with the legend of Orpheus. According to tradition, the women of the region, in a frenzy because the divine musician enchanted men, animals and trees with his melodies, killed him in the foothills of the mountain not far from Dion. After this they attempted to wash their bloodied hands in the river Helikon that flowed in the ravine of Mount Olympos. The river, however, to avoid

Relief depicting Isis, from the facade of the goddess's temple.

Statue of Isis-Tyche in the niche in the goddess's temple.

being polluted, vanished into the earth and resurfaced at Dion with a different name. From this point to its mouth it was called the Baphyras and nymphs bathed in its crystal-clear waters. This legend gives an explanation for the geological phenomenon whereby the water vanishes in the pebble bed of the ravine and reappears in the springs of Dion.

The worship of the water of Olympos seems to have been a decisive factor in the foundation

The temples in the sanctuary of Isis.

Head of the river god Baphyras.

Slab with 'foot-prints' from the steps to the temple of Isis Lochias.

on this site, as early as the Classical period, of a sanctuary dedicated to Artemis, in her capacity as goddess of child-birth. In later times a sacred spring was housed in a temple, and the water from another spring was conducted into a cistern in the temple of Aphrodite Hypolympidia ('Aphrodite of the foothills of Olympos') where it ran beneath her statue.

The excavations in the area flooded by water were conducted under very difficult conditions. On occasion, the entire project seemed Sisyphean, with huge land-slips or terrible floods covering with mud everything that had been revealed with such great effort. One addi-

Model of the sanctuary of Isis.

tional task was to move the river bed a few metres to the west in order to uncover the rest of the main temple, which was at the bottom of the river.

Work began in the summer of 1978 and revealed a sanctuary complete with its temples, altars, the stoa for visitors, rooms for the priests and many of the statues. Some of these were not fallen in front of their pedestals, but stood upright, exactly as they were in antiquity. The main entrance is at the east. Directly opposite rises the main temple with four Ionic

The sanctuary of Isis from the west.

columns on the facade. Behind these was a marble stairway leading to the pronaos and cella. A marble relief was incorporated in the facade of the temple depicting Isis holding ears of corn and a sceptre, and wearing a broad-brimmed hat on her head. On the steps to the temple were found two low statue bases, which had not been moved since antiquity, on the slabs of which were carved footprints and

The facade of the temple of Isis and the altar.

inscriptions dedicated to Isis Lochias. In front of the temple were discovered the great altar and a processional way that started from the entrance and ended at the temple. To the left of the main temple, which was devoted to Isis Lochias, the goddess who succeeded Artemis, stands a small temple of Aphrodite Hypolympidia.

The name of the goddess was incised on a statue base of dark marble, next to the entrance. The small building has a single chamber and its floor is worked into the form of a stepped cistern. The statue of Aphrodite stood in a rectangular recess in the west wall. Lower down, on the marble rim of the cistern, stood another dedication, a small altar and a circular relief depicting Aphrodite seated on a goat. The small temple was made of brick and partly revetted with marble. the unrevetted part was covered with red plaster.

The temple on the other side of the main temple was probably also connected in some way with Aphrodite, judging by the statue of Eros, part of a group of Aphrodite and Eros, found in its antechamber.

These three temples all stand on the same line and belong to the original design of this building phase in the 2nd c. AD. By contrast, the fourth temple to the south, which has a large semicircular apse at the west, was built later, as is betrayed by its different masonry and the way it is squashed into the corner of the sanctuary. During the excavation of 1979 the cult statue of the goddess was found standing on its base. It was a female figure holding a cornucopia in her left hand. This was undoubtedly a statue of the goddess Tyche (Fortune), or more precisely, as the inscription incised on the altar informs us, of Isis-Tyche. In the middle of the temple is the sacred spring, the walls

Copy of the statue of Aphrodite Hypolympidia in its recess.

Silver tetradrachm of Alexander with a depiction of Olympian Zeus. From the excavations in the sanctuary.

Royal letter from Philip V to the people of Demetrias and Pherai.

Treaty between Lysimacheia and Philip V.

of which were revetted with marble slabs when the floor was laid.

A room containing three statue bases was found in the north wing of the sanctuary. On the third base stood the statue of Julia Frugiane Alexandra, which was erected by the city of Dion. The other two bore statues of Anthestia Iucunda and her daughter Maxima. Anthestius and his wife had donated a considerable sum for the building work in this sanctuary.

According to the archaeological evidence, the sanctuary of Isis, which was originally the sanctuary of Artemis, was built in the late Classical period and completely rebuilt from the foundations towards the end of the 2nd c. AD. Both old and new statues were erected in the new buildings. The life of the sanctuary continued until the 4th c. AD, when it suffered serious damage as a result of a devastating earthquake. The priests had begun to restore the building when terrible floods and a series of further earthquakes delivered the *coup de grâce*. It seems highly likely that the major earthquake that reduced the sanctuary to ruins was the one that destroyed the earliest Christian basilica in Dion. The cult of Isis and worship of Christ seem to have continued side by side for a period at Dion. The mystic nature of the cult of the Egyptian goddess would have seemed congenial to the devotees of the new religion. The festival of Isis was held twice each year, in spring and autumn, in keeping with the commonly found practice. The initiates entered the precinct and offered sacrifices, ranging from oxen to poultry, depending on their financial means. Travelling salesmen set up makeshift tables around the precinct and sold slaves, animals, clothes, gold and silver. Entrance to the *adyton* of the temple, how-

ever, was reserved for those to whom the great goddess appeared and spoke in their sleep.

Crossing the bridge again, visitors come to a paved path leading along the side of the river to the sanctuary of Olympian Zeus, where excavations are still continuing.

The combined evidence of three inscriptions found in this sector suggest that it is to be identified with the **sanctuary of Olympian Zeus**. The first contains the text of a royal letter from Philip V, defining the boundaries line between Demetrias and Pherai in Thessaly, and the second is a decree of the city of Dion dating from the late 4th c. BC. In both inscriptions it is explicitly stated that they should be erected in the sanctuary of Olympian Zeus. The third inscription contains no such provision but, since it too is a royal letter, this time from Antigonos, it must have been erected in the same sanctuary. The buildings uncovered

Aerial photograph of the excavation in the sanctuary of Zeus.

Decree erected in the sanctuary of Zeus.

belong to various phases of the Hellenistic period. It is clear from the column fragments that they belonged to a large Doric building. A straight wall more than one hundred metres long at the west is possibly part of the sanctuary enclosure wall. Finally, fragments of sculpture and of more inscriptions make an important contribution to what we know of this major sanctuary.

A few metres to the south are the ruins of the theatre dating from the Roman imperial period. Its masonry suggests that it was built in the 2nd c. AD. The *cavea* was supported on funnel-shaped vaults. It had stone seats and there was a low pedestal running along the curved side of the semicircular orchestra. The niches in the *skene* contained statues, amongst them one depicting Hermes and another of an emperor wearing a breastplate. The **Roman theatre** now lies in a flooded area beneath the shade of tall trees. There is an enchanting view from here of Mount Olympos.

Aerial photograph of the Roman theatre.

Returning to the central point of the tour of the excavations, visitors pass a group of bathhouses which have not yet been completely excavated. On the left is the **great theatre** of Dion, where artistic events – mainly performances of ancient drama – are held in the summer. Like some other Greek theatres, that at Dion had a number of peculiar features: the spectators' seats were made of brick, and the *cavea* rested on an artificial mound of earth. Trenches dug deep into the centre of this have brought to light coins, the earliest of which is a coin of Amyntas III – that is, from the early 4th c. BC. It is probable

therefore that the theatre at which the tragedies written by Euripides in Macedonia, the *Archelaos* and the *Bacchae*, were presented, stood on the same site, though it was probably a smaller structure. One of the rare features of the theatre of Dion is the subterranean passage, which begins in the area of the *skene* and ends at an opening in the middle of the orchestra. This is the so-called Charon's ladder, from which emerged spirits from the underworld, as required by the text of some ancient plays. The water that collected in the

Aerial photograph of the Hellenistic theatre.

Plan of the Hellenistic theatre.

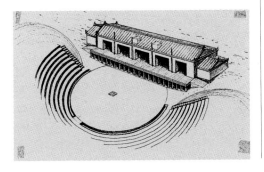

Reconstruction of the Hellenistic theatre.

31

huge cavea – a large part of which is now missing – ran into an open channel around the edge of the orchestra, from where it drained away. Next to the theatre has been found a sanctuary of Dionysos, which has yielded sculptures and an inscription, now in the Dion Museum.

Proceeding north from the central point of the tour, visitors enter the city. Very few features of the original phase of the south gate have survived, because there were radical modifications of it in later times. The entire length of the main paved road has been excavated as far as the north gate of the ancient city. The paved area is almost six metres wide, though it narrows perceptibly towards the north. Our picture of the street today is deceptive, for in the 4th and 5th c. AD it had defence wall along the west side, enclosing part of the city and converting it into a small fortress. Behind the ruins of this wall is **the great Baths complex** of Dion. In recent years ten baths complexes have been discovered and partly, at least, excavated at Dion. The great Baths, however, surpass all the others in terms of size and luxury. In the 2nd and 3rd c. AD the *Thermae*, or hot baths, were not simply bath-houses. The citizens of that period used to spend several hours almost every day at the baths, where, in addition to bathing, they had opportunities for social intercourse, the worship of the gods, physical exercise and recreation.

The staircase leading up to the courtyard of the Baths was at the end of a row of shops and workshops facing on to the main road. In the excavations deep beneath the floor of the shops can be seen the walls of buildings dating from the 4th c. BC and the Hellenistic period. At this time there was probably a large stoa on the same site as the shops. A narrow doorway

Left: the Great Baths at Dion.

33

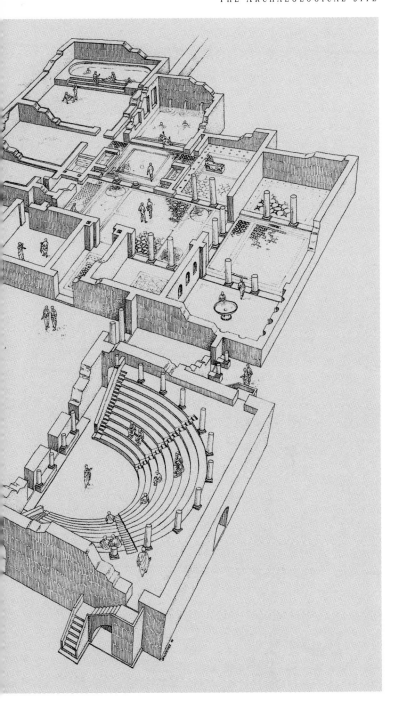

Reconstruction of the Baths.

The odeion of the Baths.

on the left of the corridor of the staircase led to the public toilets. Around the sides of the room ran a marble bench with circular holes, and directly below this was the deep sewer that collected the waste, which was flushed by running water from the bath-house. The floor had a mosaic with scenes of aquatic animals and a channel to drain off urine. In Roman times toilets of this type were usually called *Vespasianae*, as a reaction to the tax on public lavatories introduced by the emperor Vespasian.

Crossing the courtyard of the Baths, to the west, visitors come to the entrance, which was deliberately made narrow in order to control movement through it. The floor had a mosaic paving, below which was the large main conduit leading off the bath-water. Two vertical pipes conducted water from the roof to this main conduit. Beyond the entrance, one entered the great hall with the mosaic floor. At the back of this was the large pool with cold water, on the right rooms devoted to recreation and the cult of Asklepios, and on the left the rooms with tepid and hot water. Below the floor of the latter was a low, subterranean room whose roof was supported by a large number of built pillars. This underground room was the hypocaust, in which hot air circulated to heat the floor. Fire burned in furnaces specially created in the exterior wall. Hot air was not confined to the floor, but also rose in the hollows deliberately left at the centre of the walls and heated them. The rooms in which water was to be found were paved with marble slabs. The others had mosaic floors, the most brilliant of them in the antechamber to the

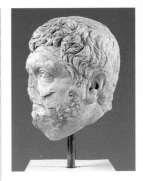

Portrait head from the large room in the Baths.

The statues of the daughters of Asklepios, from the Baths.

Panakeia, daughter of Asklepios, from the Baths.

natatio (pool); coloured tesserae are used to depict the abduction of the Nereids by the Tritons, set in a sea-scape. Of the sculptural decoration of the baths, statues have been found of Poseidon, Dionysos, a Nymph, and a group depicting Asklepios and all his family. In addition to the statues of deities, the baths contained two copies of portraits, apparently of important citizens of ancient Dion. One of these was Erennianos, who was in charge of the philosophical education of his time, and the other was an unknown, bearded man, probably a member of the city administration. From the courtyard of the Baths can be seen the odeion, a small roofed theatre in which were held musical concerts and readings of books, and which was probably also used as a council-chamber (*bouleuterion*), for the agora was directly behind it. The *cavea* of the odeion was supported on eleven funnel-shaped vaults, and crowned by a semicircle of Ionic columns. The great Baths of Dion were built about 200 AD, as part of a wider programme of new public buildings.

At the west end of the great Baths was the large cistern that fed the installations with water. Next to this can be seen the inside of the **Dion fortification walls**.

The city of Dion acquired its monumental fortifications at the end of the 4th c. BC, in the reign of Kassander. The flat, slightly sloping terrain in which the city was set was marked only be the deep beds of winter torrents and a river, and this made it possible to give the city a geometric lay-out without any great problems. The fortifications were rectangular,

Left: The statue of Dionysos from the frigidarium of the Baths.

Right: The statue of Podaleirios from the Baths.

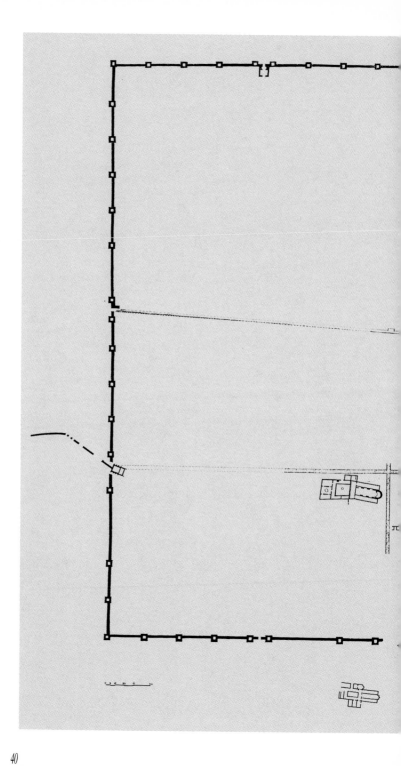

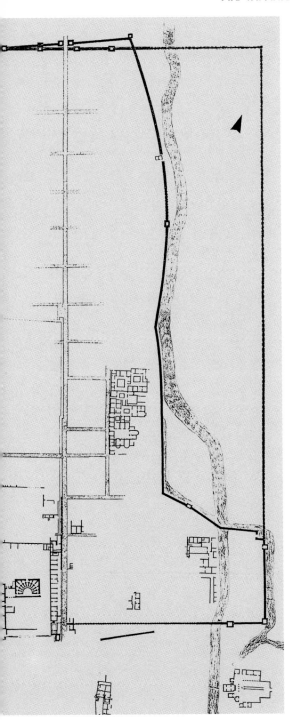

Plan of the city of
Dion.

almost square, in plan, and had a circuit of over 2600 metres. To withstand assaults and sieges, it was three metres thick and had rectangular towers at intervals of 33 metres. It was built of large blocks of conglomerate from Mount Olympos. The six gates so far excavated are located at the ends of the main arteries of the city. The best preserved is the west gate in the north wall, which is flanked by two towers and has a double interior courtyard for defen-

The tower of the west gate in the north wall.

The 3rd c. AD fortifications built on the ruins of the 4th c. BC fortifications.

sive purposes. There were large scale repairs of the fortifications after the destruction by the Aetolians at the end of the 3rd BC, and in the Roman period they were abandoned and fell into ruins. New fortifications were constructed on the ruins about the middle of the 3rd c. AD, when the city was threatened by barbarian

raids. A modification in the course of the fortifications was imposed by a change in the course of the river, which seems to have flooded part of the city to the east. Here the new fortifications followed the course of the river and were therefore irregular. The material used in this phase was rubble with courses of bricks. Wherever collapsed material from the earlier walls existed, however, this was re-used. Nor did the builders hesitate to incorporate monuments, mainly funerary altars, from the neighbouring cemetery. The defences of Dion were renovated for the final time in the Early Christian Period. At this date a large sec-

Aerial photograph of the central part of the archaeological site at Dion.

Part of the gate in the east wall.

The cemetery basilica at Dion.

tion of the east and north part of the city remained outside the fortifications. At the centre of the city, now greatly reduced in size, rose its outstanding public building, the Christian basilica.

Near the great Baths and the south fortification wall, visitors to Dion may see a charming basilica built in the 5th c. AD outside the city in the region of a cemetery dating from this period. Beneath both the sanctuary and the atrium of the basilica there are Christian tombs. One of them belonged to an elder called Andreas, while another was a cenotaph, possibly devoted to a saint named Magna. One of the tombs had wall-paintings depicting birds of paradise set amongst purple crosses. The sanctuary of this three-aisled basilica was separated off by decorative marble closure slabs affixed to pilasters. In the sanctuary apse was found the pit for the enkainion, traces of the Altar legs, and the glass lamp, along with the bronze crucifix from which it was suspended. The mosaic floor in the main aisle was decorated with geometric shapes and floral motifs.

The **main basilica** of Dion, which was undoubtedly an episcopal church, since Dion had become the seat of a bishop, was built in the second half of the 4th c. AD and destroyed shortly afterwards by a terrible earthquake before the work on it had even been completed. It was rebuilt, slightly larger, on the same site though with a difference of two metres between the floor levels. The mosaic floor of the main aisle and the narthex is preserved intact from the first building phase. From the second phase survive part of the mosaic in the north aisle and part of the marble revetment of the central aisle. The walls of the first basilica were decorated with paintings that were given architectural articulation in imitation of coloured revetment. The main entrance to the

The main basilica at Dion.

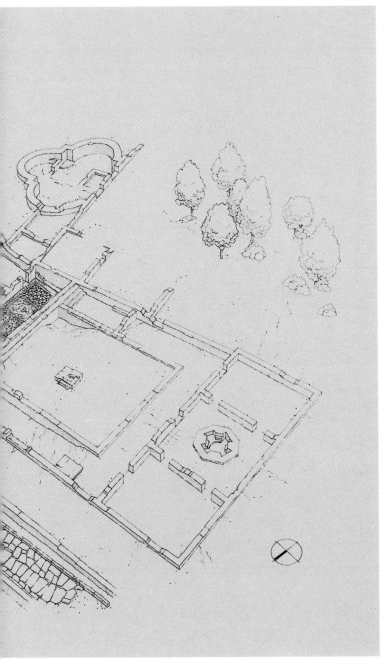

Perspective drawing
of the main basilica
of Dion.

atrium of the second basilica was from the paved road that led to the west gate in the fortification wall. In the centre of atrium was a fountain, and at its west side, in the central room of the three, is the baptistery, which has an octagonal font. Excavations to the south of the nave have uncovered a triconch building that was probably the baptistery of the first basilica. Throughout the entire complex the walls incorporated architectural members of other, earlier buildings, including colonnettes, statue bases and gravestones.

Following the road towards Mount Olympos, visitors come to the west gate in the fortification wall, about 300 metres away, where the solid 4th c. BC pilasters are still standing, as is the great city reservoir, built on this site in the 2nd c. AD. Proceeding in the opposite direction to the entrance to the basilica, towards the main street, we pass the luxurious **house of Euboulos**, which had mosaic floors, a central atrium, and a fountain in the large room next to it. The owner's name is frequently recorded

The House of
Euboulos.

in relief on the lead water pipe. Immediately beyond the house is a paved path that leads to the edge of the main square of the agora, which has the shape of square measuring approximately 60 x 60 metres. The last monumental phase of this dates to the late 2nd or early 3rd c. AD. At a depth of 3-4 metres, however, there are the ruins of buildings dating from the 4th c. BC and the Hellenistic period. From the agora comes a thick marble slab with sockets to hold bronze vessels, which was used by the market inspectors to check liquid measures. In the Early Christian period this was used in a repair of the road surface.

To the right of the intersection with the main road stands a **monument with shields and breast-plates** carved in relief. It could be seen in this position until the final days of the life of the city, but it dates from many centuries earlier, at the end the 4th c. BC. It was a total length of 37 metres and originally either formed the base of a large monument to Nike or adorned the wall of a public building. A large Baths is being excavated directly opposite

Aerial photograph of the main street, the monument of the shields, and part of the agora.

and, on the same axis though at the level of the agora and some distance to the west, a single-chamber building has been excavated that contained statues of emperors.

To the south of the monument with the shields can be seen parts of large buildings dating from the end of the Classical period and early Hellenistic times. A road that started from the east marble gate in the fortifications led to this precise spot.

To the left of the intersection a paved road leads along the late fortification wall, which at this point was built almost exclusively of

The large atrium of the Villa of Dionysos.

dozens of column drums taken from Hellenistic buildings, to a number of building blocks that have been partially excavated. In the second of these, excavations are revealing a building complex in which some of the rooms contained many iron and bronze tools and a number of small *objets d'art*. A bronze speculum dating from the 1st c. AD and the famous

bronze *hydraulis* ('organ') of Dion were both found here. Directly opposite is the **villa of Dionysos**.

Excavation of the villa complex began in the summer of 1982. A row of shops came to light on the facade, and also the residence rooms, the large banquet room, the cult area, the atria, the library and the large bath-house.

The main entrance was on the left side and led through a small antechamber to a courtyard with a well. The roof of the stoa encircling this courtyard was supported by four Ionic

Aerial photograph of part of the Villa of Dionysos.

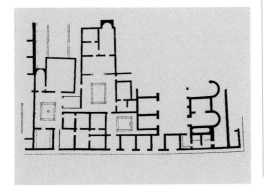

Plan of the central section of the Villa of Dionysos.

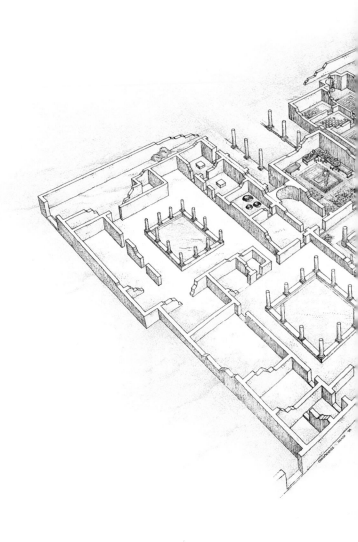

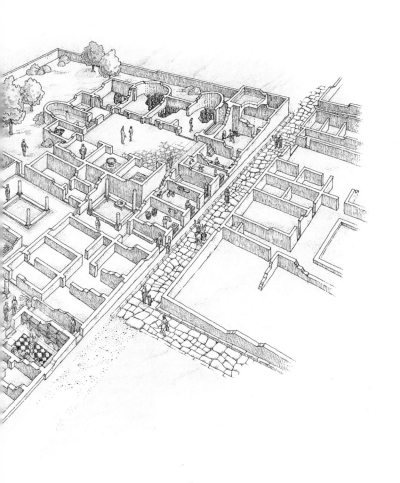

Reconstruction of the villa of Dionysos.

columns. A corridor led to the baths, and a
doorway to the main atrium which had a water
cistern in the centre. From here a large opening at the east, flanked by two columns, led to
a group of small rooms. The largest of these,
which was elongated in plan and had an apse

at the east end, contained the statue of Dionysos, with a mosaic in front of it depicting the god enthroned, holding a sceptre in his hand, and wearing an ivy wreath on his head. This was probably a small temple devoted to the cult of the god and incorporated into the

The philosophers from the Villa of Dionysos.

Dionysos.

Young sea centaur
with a closed vase
on his shoulder.

Sea centaur holding
a krater.

The mosaic of the banquet room in the Villa of Dionysos.

Detail of the mosaic.

villa complex. A corridor at the north connected the main atrium with a second much more luxuriously constructed court, which had its own separate entrance from the street. The finest of the sculptures decorating the building were found in this courtyard and the rooms around it. Most importantly, however, it was this atrium that gave access to the great banqueting room, whose mosaic floor, roughly one hundred square metres in size, was preserved intact. Along three of the walls the mosaic was bordered by as broad band, where the couches were placed. This band is followed by the impressive zone with the frieze, in which tendrils with flowers and acanthus calyxes are portrayed against a dark ground. Within this zone is set the panel with the main scene, which is flanked by six smaller ones depicting theatrical masks. In the main scene Dionysos stands on the box of his chariot, wearing an ivy wreath and holding a thyrsus in one hand and a winecup in the form of an animal horn in the other. Next to him he supports an aged Silenos wearing a woollen *chiton* and a short, purple *himation*. The scene depicts a triumphal epiphany of the god, who emerges from the waves of the sea riding on a chariot pulled by two sea panthers. Two sea centaurs lead these fantastic monsters by the reins: one of them is of mature age with a beard, and carries a silver krater on his back, while the other is a clean-shaven youth, who holds a closed vase which probably contained the secret symbols of the cult of Dionysos. This mosaic panel, with its delicate coloured tesserae, is of an unusually high quality. There is no doubt that it is a masterpiece of mosaic art. The same is true of the smaller panels. The central one of these, depicting a mask of the god, is flanked by two other masks. One portrays a satyr projected against a drum, and the other an aged man who has the ancient conventional appearance of a barbarian; it was probably a depiction of Lykourgos, the king of Thrace, who attempted to prevent the establishment of the worship of Dionysos, but was punished for it by the Olympian gods. The three masks on the west side were those of a young satyr, a young woman and an aged Silenos. The last of these three is the most unusual and also has the most powerful expression. It probably depicts the wise Silenos whom King Midas persuaded, with great difficulty, to teach him the secrets of his knowledge. On the floor of

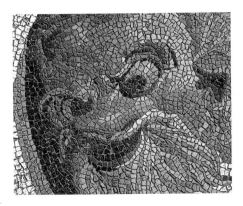

Mask of a satyr from the banquet room in the Villa of Dionysos.

the banquet room were found the decorative bronze attachments of a couch: two busts of horses for the crowning member and two circular busts to decorate the curving base of the supports. This couch will have been a rare piece of antique furniture, already at least two centuries old when it was used in this room. During the excavation of this area, four more headless statues of philosophers were found which had been temporarily placed on the mosaic floor. Without doubt they had been brought here from elsewhere. Indeed, during the excavation of the atrium, three of the heads for the statues were found. The removal of these headless statues may be accounted for by an attempt to remove what could be saved from the atrium, which had probably been destroyed by an earthquake. Moreover, building material for the repair work had been assembled inside the banqueting room. A terrible fire swept the villa, however, and put an end to the life of the building. In the north wall of the atrium associated with the banqueting room was a marble aedicule, in which was erected a superb statuette of Herakles with a stag next to him. In the centre of the atrium is a well with a marble cover, in which there were fragments of sculpture, and glass and wooden vases. To the west of the atrium is a room which has a luxury marble floor and low arcades along the walls which probably supported wooden book-shelves. The two large building units to the north with the dodecastyle courtyards were originally connected with the villa but later became independent of it. Particular interest attaches to a room with an earthen floor on which fragments of the mosaic floor from the first storey collapsed in a heap.

A group of residences being excavated at the south end of the city is of particular interest. The finds here include a large number of rooms paved with mosaic floors. One large room also contained some superb table legs, with the table top itself, with depictions of a lion's head, Dionysos, and Leda and the Swan.

To the west of the entrance building to the excavations can be seen the **retaining wall of the ancient stadium**. Investigations to date have located the original slope of the embankment, the end of the track, and the channel to drain off the rain water. The discovery of the stadium is of particular importance because this was the area in which the ancient Macedonians held the Dion Olympic Games.

The uncovering of two marble heads in the south room of the small atrium in the Villa of Dionysos.

ΧΑΡΙΤΙΝ ΜΑΞΙΜΩ
Ω ΓΛΥΚΥΤΑΩ ΑΝΔΡΙ
ΙΝ ΚΑΛΩΝ ΒΙΩΝ ΜΥΟΙ
ΧΑΡΙ ΕΜΑΣ ΘΑΣ
ΕΦΙΛΗΣΑ ΑΘΩΠΝ
ΝΚΑ ΦΙΛΟΥΣ ΛΗΣΗΤ
ΡΙΣ ΟΙΔΕ ΜΟΔΙ
ΠΑΜΠΟΛΕΩ
ΦΙΛΕΤΕΝ ΙΣΕΜΑΣ
ΤΗΝ ΧΑΡΙΤΑΝ

3/8/95
Ιωαννίδου Χριστίνα

THE MUSEUM

The courtyard. As visitors enter the courtyard of the museum they see a group of marble altars on the right. These are so-called Macedonian altars, which used to be placed above tombs in the 2nd and 3rd c. AD. In most cases the monument is decorated by a pine cone. This has a metaphorical significance. The seeds that will grow in them indicated the life that continues. Some of the inscriptions are very laconic. Others are particularly charming, like one for a woman whose nickname was 'Charitle' (Grace), and another in which one of the dead man's lady friends says: 'I love him, I loved him, I have loved him. Only Aphrodite knows that he loved me.' A large altar in the middle of an exedra with a bilingual inscription was dedicated to one Pyrilampes, who was of noble descent. He died at the early age of 23, and his body has been delivered up, according to the inscription, to the soil of Macedonia.

Left: the grave altar of Charite.

The entrance to Macedonian Tomb IV.

Early Iron Age grave tumulus at Mesonisi, before excavation.

Directly opposite the altar of Pyrilampes is another large altar possibly also dating from the 1st c. AD, which was brought from Dion to the coast at Katerini in order to travel to Constantinople during the Balkan wars. For some unknown reason, however, it went no further. It was photographed and drawn by English archaeologists and returned to Dion when the museum was built. Behind it a genuine tumulus has been constructed using authentic material from an extensive Early Iron Age (1000-700 BC) cemetery just outside Dion, in the foothills of Mount Olympos. A section cut in the main body of the tumulus

Vases in an Early Iron Age tomb.

The tumulus after excavation.

Bronze spectacle fibula.

and the ground enables visitors to see the tombs and to understand their relationship with the mound. It is a low tumulus and precisely at the centre can be seen the *sema* (marker), a large, upright stone. The tombs, made of schist slabs, contained the skeleton of the deceased and the grave offerings. The excavation of the cemetery leaves one with the impression that the tombs were placed around a central one containing a male burial. Frequently the same tomb was used for a later burial, after the bones had been removed. The vases were placed near the head and the legs. In female

Typical skyphos with Geometric decoration from the tumulus at Mesonisi.

burials, bronze spectacle fibulae and large pins used to fasten and adorn clothing were frequently found at shoulder level. Traces of settlements dating from this period have also been found in the foothills of Mount Olympos outside the cemetery. The finds from the cemeteries in the slopes of Olympos at this date exhibit great similarity with similar discoveries from Vergina and Thessaly. This sheds some historical light on the mythical account of Hesiod, who, about 700 BC, speaks of the two brothers, who were sons of Olympian Zeus, Makedon and Magnes, each of whom gave their name to their land.

The marble leaves from the door of Macedonian tomb I have been set upright in the museum portico. The tomb itself is outside the west gate in the fortifications. Its white facade was decorated with a zone of triglyphs and metopes. The antechamber is articulated by slender Ionic half-columns flanking the doorway leading into the main chamber. Here were found the marble door-leaves which have been mended and conserved. Inside the chamber there is a marble funerary couch. The legs of the couch were decorated by geometric shapes and the broad transverse beams connecting them had a coloured battle scene. This tomb dates from the late 4th c. BC and obviously belonged to a rich Macedonian official.

Another Macedonian tomb (IV) has been excavated in a high tumulus in the nearby village of Karitsa. A built *dromos* leads to its entrance. In this case the marble door-leaves are still *in situ*. The tomb dates from the end of the 3rd c. BC. A total of five Macedonia tombs have been excavated in the region of Dion.

As visitors proceed towards the entrance to the

The facade of
Macedonian Tomb I.

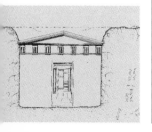

museum, they can also see a marble table in the portico, supported on the head and leg of a lion. Table tops like these have only rarely been found. This one is decorated with two confronted busts of eagles. High tables like this were used to display the valuable vessels used at banquets.

Ground floor. In the large room on the ground floor are exhibited groups of finds from **the great baths, the sanctuary of Isis**, and **the sanctuary of Demeter**.

The large marble basin and the statues behind it were found in the same room in the baths. The basin was found roughly in the centre of the room, while the statues probably stood in niches. Inscriptions on the statue bases helped to identify them securely. The names that can be read are Machaon, Hygeia, Aigle, Panakeia,

Sculptures in the main room on the ground-floor, from the Baths and the sanctuary of Isis.

Akeso and Podaleirios. All six were children of Asklepios. This is the first time that we have an almost complete set of the statues of the children of Asklepios. Only fragments have been found of the statue of Asklepios himself. These sculptures came from a Neo-attic workshop of the 2nd c. AD, and reproduce statue types of the early Hellenistic period.

The statue of Dionysos at the left, with a small satyr next to him, was found in the *natatio* of the Bath-house, and probably stood in one of the niches in the walls overlooking the water. Traces of paint are preserved in the god's hair and the animal's skin. It is a 2nd c. AD work based on 4th c. BC models.

The hermaic stele of Errenianos is a masterpiece of ancient portraiture. The head was found in a shop associated with the villa, and the main body of the stele in the baths. It depicts a mature man with delicate features and well-groomed hair. The eyes are turned slightly upwards, indicating something of his spirituality. The epigram carved on it, in Homeric language, contains a charming pun indicating that there was another portrait of the same man, of which a fragment was in fact found during the excavation of the Baths. It dates from the early 3rd c. AD, and is a representative example of the revival of Classical civilisation at this period. Next to it are two portraits of the same man. They are identical in every detail, but of different quality, which suggests that one was the model and the other a copy. They date from the early 3rd c. AD and were found in the Baths.

Finds from the sanctuary of Isis. The marble head at the left probably came from the cult statue of the goddess in the main temple. A

The hermaic stele of Erennianos. The head was taken in antiquity from the baths to the Villa of Dionysos.

relief with a votive inscription naming the triad of Sarapis, Isis and Anubis, and dating from the 2nd c. BC, is the earliest testimony to the cult of the goddess Isis at Dion. The statue, on its ancient base, stood in a niche of the temple of Isis-Tyche. It dates to around AD 200. The base is here in third use. Originally it bore a large statue depicting king Kassander of Macedonia The inscription preserved on the top surface is as follows:

The cult statue of Isis-Tyche on its pedestal.

Inscription from the first use of the pedestal of the statue of Isis-Tyche.

KING OF THE MACEDONIANS
KASSANDER SON OF ANTIPATER
TO OLYMPIAN ZEUS

This statue probably stood in the sanctuary of Zeus and may have belonged to one of the portraits of the king overturned by the Aetolian general Skopas at the end of the 3rd c. BC

Two marble models of bulls found near the altar may conceivably have been connected

Statue of Poseidon
from the sanctuary
of Isis-Tyche.

with the Egyptian god Apis. The three small
female busts were set in the same order on a
low wall at the side of the corridor leading to
the entrance to the altar. They may represent a
triad of goddesses. The two statuettes of children depict the young Harpokrates, compan-
ion of Isis, and the slabs with 'footprints' were
dedications to the goddess. The large and
small footprints belong respectively to a man
and a woman. In inscriptions on the island of

The statue of Aphrodite Hypolympidia.

Delos, similar footprints are called *bemata* (steps). They were obviously dedications made by pilgrims visiting the sanctuary who had travelled a long way to reach the steps leading to the temple where these votives were erected. Directly opposite is a large pedestal on which stand a statue of Poseidon with a dolphin and an octopus as supports, and an archaistic statuette of Artemis, with the base of another statue next to it, dedicated by Aristio, daughter of Mentor to Artemis Eileithyia, the goddess of child-birth. Artemis is the goddess who came from her great temple at Ephesos to the palace at Pella to assist at the birth of Alexander the Great.

The charming statue of Aphrodite Hypolympidia stands on a separate pedestal. She was

Statue of Aphrodite from the area of the altar in the sanctuary of Isis Lochias.

the local Aphrodite worshipped at Dion, and her cult was connected with the waters of Olympos. She wears a translucent chiton, girded directly below the breasts, as was the fashion in the Hellenistic period. The himation hangs loosely at the lower part of the body and is gathered on the right leg. The body is relaxed, for the goddess is leaning against a tree trunk. This 2nd c. BC sculpture broke and was repaired in the 2nd c. AD, when it was placed on a new base, on which was incised a Latin inscription stating that the dedicator was Anthestia Iucunda. The small altar, the circular relief depicting Aphrodite on a goat, and the relief with the cockerel, one of the goddess's favourite animals, stood in front of the statue on the marble ledge of the small temple.

Statue of the goddess Demeter from the sanctuary of Isis.

Statue of Harpokrates from the sanctuary of Isis.

Opposite stands another small Hellenistic statue of Aphrodite. These were found near the large altar in the sanctuary of Isis.

The bases for the statues of Anthestia Iucunda and her daughter Maxima, and the statue of Julia Frugiane Alexandra have been placed in exactly the same order in which they were found in the sanctuary. A Greek translation was inscribed beneath the Latin inscriptions on the first two, for, as is clear from funerary inscriptions of the period, the vast majority of the population spoke Greek even during the Roman Empire. This group of finds associated with Isis closes with the small statue of Demeter sitting on the *cista mystica*, dating from the late 4th c. BC, with the mill-stone and fruit-press for ritual use.

Finds from the sanctuary of Demeter. The long narrow pedestal supports the marble head of the goddess Demeter found in the cella of her temple. The small holes indicate the places where her diadem and earrings, which were probably made of gilded bronze, were attached. The other head at the end of the pedestal was found together with the altar in question, which has an inscription giving the name of the priestess of Aphrodite. The worship of Aphrodite in a sanctuary devoted to female fertility deities is not surprising. The statues were found in the late 4th c. BC temples and date from the Hellenistic period.

The showcase contains a representative collection of small finds: terracotta figurines dating from as early as the beginning of the 5th c. BC, lamps from the same period and later, a group of terracotta figurine-heads found buried in the same small pit, jewellery made of gold, bronze and glass, such as the precious glass vase (half of which survives) in the form of a shallow cup for liquid offerings to the gods.

Opposite is a reconstruction of the offering table dedicated, according to the inscription, by Menekrite, priestess of Baubo, a mythical figure from the Eleusinian cycle.

A Hellenistic statue of a Muse holding a lyre, the sound-box of which is an imitation of a tortoise shell, stands apart at the back of the room. It probably depicts Terpsichore standing on a rock.

Going towards the back of the room, visitors come to a case on the right containing a variety of small finds: the head of a small child wearing a hood (this is the healing spirit Telesphoros), a 5th c. BC seal-ring with a depiction of Eros from the sanctuary of Asklepios, a por-

The statue of Julia Frugiane Alexandra from the sanctuary of Isis.

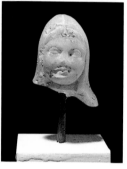

Head of Asklepios from the god's sanctuary.

Head of Telesphoros from the sanctuary of Asklepios.

trait of a ruler from the bottom of a clay vase found beneath the foundations of the *skene* of the Roman theatre, a small head of Isis and a figure of Sarapis.

Opposite stands a superb statuette of Hygeia, a masterful 2nd c. AD rendering of a known work of the Classical period. A snake slithers down the goddess's back towards her hand.

The head of a youth with long curling tresses immediately after this depicts the river god of Dion, Baphyras. Traces of the depiction of the city walls survive on the top part of the head.

On the large pedestal immediately after this is the lower part of an impressive sculpture depicting the goddess Nemesis standing on a female personification of Injustice. Next to it are the Balance of Justice and the Wheel of Fortune.

Statue of a Muse.

Statue of Hygeia from the sanctuary of Asklepios.

Head of Zeus.

Statue of a Hermaphrodite from the sanctuary of Dionysos.

On the pedestal opposite is a collection of finds mainly from the sanctuary of Dionysos, outstanding amongst them being the Hellenistic statue of a Hermaphrodite. This bisexual figure, combining the characteristics of both sexes, symbolised fertility in the cycle of the worship of Dionysos.

The head with a long beard probably represents Zeus, the father of the gods. This work acts as an introduction to the inscriptions that follow. They come from the precinct and sanctuary of Olympian Zeus. One of them contains the text of a late 4th c. BC decree, by which the city of Dion accords the privilege of *proedria* ('front-row seats') at the athletic and dramatic contests. The beginning, which would have informed us who the ruler was whose portrait it was decided to erect in front of the temple of Zeus, is unfortunately missing. The next

Depiction of Medea decorating a table-support.

inscription is precisely dated to the 16th year of the reign of Philip V (= 206 BC) and refers to the settling of a boundary dispute between Demetrias and Pherai. The text gives explicit instructions to erect the inscription in the precinct of Olympian Zeus. The third inscription is carved in large letters on the base of the marble statue of Perseus. When restored this would have been 'King Perseus, son of King Philip'. The text of the fourth inscription is a

Grave stele from
the middle of the
5th c. BC.

treaty of alliance between Philip V and the
people of Lysimacheia. Like all the previous
inscriptions, it was probably erected in the
precinct of Zeus, which was the official place
for the 'publication' of royal documents and
the display of royal statues.

The sculpture in the middle of the room
depicts Medea, in the centre, preparing to per-
petrate the tragic murder of her children, one
of whom is clinging to the bosom of a nurse.
Good quality sculpture from a Neo-attic work-

Ivory head from
Macedonian Tomb
IV.

Gold finger-ring
from the *dromos* of
Macedonian Tomb
IV, with a depiction
of Eros on the
bezel.

shop.

The two large showcases contain finds from **the cemeteries of Dion**, dating from the Classical period to late Roman times. Particular importance attaches to the group of grave offerings from Macedonian tomb IV of Dion, which include gold jewellery and ivory figures.

The funeral monuments that follow fall in the same broad chronological framework. The stele of a dead girl in the centre is a charming 5th c. BC work made by a Macedonian workshop with influences from island art. The yellowish grave stone from the late 5th c. BC bears the earliest inscription from Dion known so far: Theotimos son of Parmenon.

Funeral altar inscribed 'Theotimos Parmenionos'. Late 5th c. BC.

Grave stele of the
nun Epiktese. 5th c.
AD.

Christian grave
stone of Alexandros
and Severina.

In the corner of the room devoted to Early Christian finds are displayed objects from the basilicas, relief closure slabs, and funeral stelai. It is worth dwelling before the small marble stele at the end of the room, of a young nun whose parents were from Thessaloniki and Athens. The text, which is spare but full of sentiment, is almost reminiscent of the poetry of Cavafy.

At the end of the ground floor corridor is a stand with three panels of coins. One of them contains coins of the Macedonian kings, the second coins minted by Dion in the imperial period, and the third coins issued by other cities and found at Dion.

Grave relief of a
Roman official.

First floor. A specially designed room is devoted to the display of the unique find of the **hydraulis of Dion**, which was found in the 1992 excavations. The *hydraulis* was a musical instrument invented by the engineer Ktesibios at Alexandria in the 3rd c. BC. A row of bronze pipes of differing lengths and with a special opening near the conical base to produce the sound vibration was set on a box, which contained a mechanism designed to prevent or permit the passage of air with the assistance of keys. Air under pressure from pumps passed through water and ended at this box. In the Dion find are preserved the bronze pipes and the plaques of which they were made. There are 27 pipes up to 1.20 m. in length and with a diameter of about 2 cm., and 16 pipes with half this diameter. Both sets were placed in the same line. The pipes are supported and decorated by silver rings. The front of the outer metal plaque is relieved by silver strips. One of the polychrome glass plaques, worked in the *millefiori* technique, which were attached to the same side, also survives. The find from Dion dates from the 1st c. BC and is the earliest example of the *hydraulis*, which was the forerunner of the church organ of the West. It was very popular in Hellenistic and Roman times and was adopted at the imperial court of Byzantium. It was forgotten in the West because of the barbarian invasions, but returned there in AD 757, in the form of a gift from the Byzantine emperor.

Another very important ancient instrument became known for the first time as the result of a find made in the 1994 excavations. A funerary stele depicts an instrument resembling a harp or kithara. It has six strings, with

Left: the *hydraulis* of Dion.

85

The *nabla* of Dion.

Bust of a horse from a couch in the Villa of Dionysos.

two more at the sides to tune it, two small columns at the ends and a sound box at the bottom. This unusual instrument is the *nabla* mentioned in the ancient sources; a very ancient eastern instrument found in the temple of Solomon, the *nabla* was used by Greeks in their banquets and by Romans at a variety of celebrations. Its name is recorded in the Latin form, *nabilium*. The dead woman here, who in her life time had been a devotee of the Muses, played music on this instrument. Her husband was a man of letters, as is clear from the open papyrus depicted on the stele and as is stated explicitly in the inscription.

The next corner contains a temporary display of some of the objects found in the villa of

Dionysos, including bronze busts of horses, of Herakles, and of a Satyr, which are all masterpieces of Macedonian metal-working of the late Hellenistic period. Also displayed here are a statuette of Herakles and a stag, which is a superb copy of a Classical model, and a portrait of Agrippina, one of the best examples of its type.

Bust of a satyr from a couch in the Villa of Dionysos.

Bust of Herakles as Omphale from a couch in the Villa of Dionysos.

The statues of philosophers found in the villa have been set on a semicircular pedestal. All four are seated on thrones with their feet resting on footstools, in almost identical poses.

All of them hold a scroll in their left hand. The fourth has his scroll unrolled, probably because he was reading something. This philosopher differs from the others; with his long hair and beard he represents the image of an Epicurean philosopher in contrast with the others who all have the typical coiffure of the first half of the 3rd c. BC. Observation of the details reveals that the heads with short hair are the product of a reworking and are therefore smaller in size than one would expect. This was, then, originally a group of statues of philosophers, which were radically reworked

Showcase with finds
from the Early Iron
Age (1000-750 BC).

Two heads from the Villa of Dionysos: a copy of an idealistic 5th c. BC original, and a 2nd c. AD portrait.

and the portraits changed, and it is not impossible that they depicted some of the inhabitants of the villa. In this case, the philosopher with the open scroll will be the teacher.

The model of the area of Mount Olympos and Pieria gives a relief picture of the form of the terrain. It also illustrates clearly the course of the road arteries, and the silting up of the plains by the alluvium from the mountains, which changed the coastline.

Grave stele depicting a family whose children were drowned in a shipwreck, as can be seen from the overturned ship.

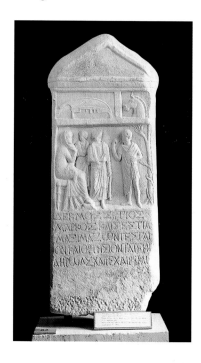

Right: Statue of Dionysos from the aedicule in the Villa of Dionysos.

The stele of Alkimachos, from the family of Olympias.

Bottom part of a grave relief with scenes from country life.

The stele at the left comes from the village of Koukos. Its surface is divided into two relief panels. The one at the top contains three busts – members of a single family. The lower panel depicts a man mounted on horseback and a ship. The former panel follows the preferences of the Roman imperial period to which the stele is dated, while the latter follows the typical Hellenistic tradition. The names, too, are indicative: Parmenion, Antigonos, and Philippe.

The finds from this point onwards come from the archaeological horizon of Dion, Pieria, the most important centre of which was Pydna, where the large funerary stele depicting a mother, child and cockerel was found. This was one of the masterpieces of sculpture in northern Greece, which kept abreast of the development of the art in the south. The child's body nestles against his mother, and their hands are linked in a tender circle. The sentimental content is moderated by the carefree gesture of the child who holds a piece of

Grave stele of the
4th c. BC from
Kitros in Pieria.

Inscription of
Apollo Dekadryos
from Pydna.

Stele of the adher-
ents of Zeus
Hypsistos.

bread in front of the bird's beak. It dates from
the second half of the 5th c. BC.

The showcases contain grave offerings and
other finds from Pydna: 5th and 4th c. BC
vases, a superb gold wreath, jewellery, and lead
sling-shot.

A large stele speaks of an unknown man from
another sanctuary of Apollo Dekadryos at
Pydna.

Two interesting stelai, one of the 4th and the
other of the 2nd c. BC, come from Kitros in
Pieria. The first depicts a young hunter with
his dog. The sculptor worked the marble sensi-
tively and rendered his figures with soft vol-
umes. On the second is depicted a mounted
Macedonian and his groom, with his wife and
her serving maid in front of them. The snake in
the tree gives the scene a chthonic and funerary character. The name of the horseman is
Philippos son of Hippotos.

The small showcase at the back of the room
contains a group of bronze finds from Ritini in
Pieria: a small bronze figurine of a kouros,
bronze models of domestic animals, a superb

Marble krater from Pydna.

figure of Eros Enagonios dating from the Classical period (the sockets for the wings are preserved), a statuette of Herakles wrestling with the Nemean lion, and another statuette depicting the same hero in a relaxed stance with his club on his shoulder and a cup in his hand, probably after drinking wine. The final group on the first floor is devoted to Iron Age finds from the foothills of Mount Olympos just outside Dion, and the highly important finds from the sanctuary of Zeus on the peak of Ayios Andonios.

The offerings from Iron Age tombs come from tumulus cemeteries at Ayios Vasilios and Mesonnisi. The most popular vase shapes are kraters, skyphoi, and oinochoai with cut-away necks. The surface of the vase is frequently painted with a light brown or red lacqueur. The decoration, where it exists, is geometric with a special preference for concentric semi-circles. The metal finds are bronze spectacle fibulae and large pins, which were used to fasten and adorn clothing. Bronze spiral bracelets and necklaces of sard were amongst the female jewellery commonly found. An iron knife was frequently deposited as an offering in male graves. The chronological context for these finds is 1000-700 BC.

The ruins of ancient buildings have occasionally been reported at various sites on the peaks of Olympos. The most important finds, however, are those from the peak of Ayios Andonios (only 100 metres lower than the highest peak of Olympos). They came to light in 1961 when the University of Thessaloniki decided to build a meteorological observatory there. The finds in question are marble stelai, sculptural fragments, potsherds, coins dating from the Hellenistic to the Byzantine periods, and above all a large number of remains of animal sacrifices. The mention of the name of Olympian Zeus in inscriptions from this same group of finds leaves no doubt that we are dealing with a sanctuary of Zeus on the peaks of Olympos, which is dated at the latest to Hellenistic period onwards.

Statue of a young
warrior from the
Villa of Dionysos.

Statue of a young
satyr at the moment
of discovery.

The large basement. A grant from the A. G.
Leventis Foundation has made it possible to
mount an educational exhibition here devoted
to daily life in ancient Dion. The exhibition is
directed not only at school children and students but also to all those visitors who would
like to form some idea of daily life in antiquity.
The first group in the exhibition contains models of the sanctuaries of Demeter and of Isis,
which help visitors to form an overall view of
the buildings, and to compare them with one
another. A sacrifice on an altar is depicted in a
relief. The priest at the right is preparing to
throw incense on the fire from a small box he
holds in his hands. The sacrificial animal
stands front of the altar, while the horseman
on the other side of it is the hero who is being

Model of part of
the Villa of
Dionysos.

honoured by the sacrifice.

The second unit presents a model of the city of
Dion, miniature reconstructions of ancient furniture, tools, precision instruments, weights,
locks, keys and two bronze supports, that were
attached to the axles of a travelling carriage.

Relief depicting a
sacrifice.

Funeral altar with depictions of wood-working tools.

The body of the carriage was suspended from the supports by leather straps.

The next subject is the alphabet and inscriptions. There is a panel showing the development of the Greek alphabet from the Phoenician and its further evolution into the Latin alphabet. Another panel presents the letter forms found in inscriptions from Dion from the 5th c. BC to the 5th c. AD. The map shows the ancient dialects and the sites in Macedonia where the earliest inscriptions have been found. Visitors may try to read a few words on fragmentary inscriptions.

In the fourth unit the large map shows the course of Alexander the Great's march, the cities he founded, the mints at which coins issued by Alexander were struck, and the sites at which coins of Philip and imitations of them have been found.

There follows a panel showing the tools of a traditional marble worker. The showcase contains ancient tools. On the bench is a demonstration of the way in which points were trans-

Hypocaust from a bath-house.

ferred from the model to the final marble work during its carving.

The theme of the sixth unit is mosaic floors and wall-paintings. A series of panels shows how mosaic and wall-paintings are detached, conserved and restored. the technique by which mosaics are made can be seen in the corner of a room, which has been restored with complete accuracy for this exhibition.

The following unit deals with the use of fire and the heating of floors and walls. Hot air rose – from an opening in the wall of the basement in which the fire burned – and heated the floor of the room above from beneath, while the double wall allowed the hot air to rise higher to the upper stories of the building.

The final unit is devoted to the water-supply and drainage systems. Terracotta and lead pipes, bronze water-taps, wells, built conduits, and prefabricated well-walls are some of the means used by the ancients to exploit water.

Water was used by ancient Greeks both for their daily needs, and also to embellish their lives by the sight and sound of it in fountains and *Nymphaia*.

Supports for the body of the travelling carriage.

Table support with a depiction of Herakles.

Satellite photograph of Mount Olympos and Pieria. The snow-covered Macedonian Olympos, 2197 m. high, can be seen at the bottom, with the lower, Thessalian Olympos and mouth of the river Peneios immediately to the south. Above the Atherida promontory, with its salt flats, lies Pydna. Further north is Methone, followed by the mouths of the Haliakmon, Loudias, Axios and Gallikos rivers.

Dion lies immediately to the left of the deep Enipeus gorge, which penetrates the heart of Olympos.

I extend my thanks to G. Karadedos, professor of Architecture and the architects M. Boliaritis, G. Orkopoulos, A. Pallis and Th. Tsironis, for the drawings and models. And to G. Poupis and M. Skiadaresis for the photographs. The aerial photographs and the photographs of the excavation are by the author.

The book «Dion» by Dimitrios Pandermalis was printed in February 1997 for Adam Editions.

Translation: David A. Hardy
Design: Th. Anagnostopoulos, Th. Presvytis
Production: Pergamos SA